GW00467564

Ami Ami Dogs 2

MORE SERIOUSLY CUTE CROCHET!

BY MITSUKI HOSHI

HARPER DESIGN
An Imprint of HarperCollins Publishers

AMI AMI DOGS 2
Copyright © 2011 Mitsuki Hoshi
Original Japanese language edition published by EDUCATIONAL FOUNDATION BUNKA
GAKUEN BUNKA PUBLISHING BUREAU
English translation rights arranged with EDUCATIONAL FOUNDATION BUNKA GAKUEN
BUNKA PUBLISHING BUREAU, Tokyo through Nippon Shuppan Hanbai Inc.

First published in 2011 by:
Harper Design
An Imprint of HarperCollins*Publishers*
10 East 53rd Street
New York, NY 10022
Tel.: (212) 207-7000
Fax: (212) 207-7654
harperdesign@harpercollins.com
www.harpercollins.com

Distributed throughout the world by:
HarperCollins*Publishers*
10 East 53rd Street
New York, NY 10022
Fax: (212) 207-7654

HarperCollins books may be purchased for educational, business, or
sales promotional use. For information, please write: Special Markets Department,
HarperCollins*Publishers*, 10 East 53rd Street, New York, NY 10022.

Book Design: Tomoko Okayama, Andrew Pothecary
Cover Design: Andrew Pothecary
Photography: Yasuo Nagumo
Line Drawing: day studio (Satomi Dairaku)
English Translation: Seishi Maruyama
Copyediting: Alma Reyes
Publisher of Original Japanese Edition: Sunao Onuma
Editor of Original Japanese Edition: Norie Hirai
Chief Editor and Production: Rico Komanoya (ricorico)

Library of Congress Control Number: 2010941622

ISBN: 978-0-06206724-1

All rights reserved. No part of this book may be used or reproduced in any
manner whatsoever without written permission except in the case of brief
quotations embodied in critical articles and reviews. For information, address
Harper Design, 10 East 53rd Street, New York, NY 10022.

Printed in China
First printing in English, 2011

Pictured on previous page:
Dalmatian (See pages 12 and 54.)

Contents

Chihuahua

(See page 47.)

Jack Russell Terrier

(See pages 30 and 45.)

Toy Poodle

(See page 50.)

Shih Tzu

(See page 52.)

Dalmatian

(See page 54.)

Papillon

(See page 56.)

Boston Terrier

(See page 58.)

Bernese Mountain Dog

(See page 60.)

Hokkaido Dog

(See page 62.)

Japanese Shiba

(See page 64.)

Bull Terrier

(See page 66.)

Magnets

(See page 68.)

Cellular Phone Accessories

(See page 70.)

Basic Crocheting Techniques

The same general crocheting method is used for creating all the dogs in this book. If you can crochet a Jack Russell Terrier, for example, you can use the same technique for the other dogs. Just follow the crocheting diagrams for each type of dog. Change the thickness of the thread to alter the sizes of the dogs.

Seated dog

approx. 2.76 in

Standing dog

approx. 3.54 in

approx. 3.54 in

approx. 3.54 in

Materials

Body: Brown and white bulky thread,
    synthetic cotton
Eyes: Black plastic sewing buttons,
    2 pieces, 0.24 in
Nose: Black nose round button,
    1 piece, 0.47 in

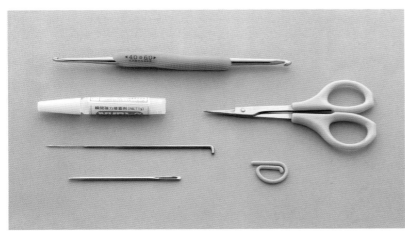

Tools

Crochet hook No. 4/0
Glue
Scissors
Felting needle (only for the Dalmatian)
Wool needle
Ring stitch markers

Thickness of threads and crochet hooks

Small dog (height: approx. 2.36 in) and
medium dog strap (height: approx. 2.16 in) =
light thread, crochet hook No. 3/0 or 2/0

Small dog strap (height: approx.1.38 in) =
fine thread, crochet hook No. 2/0

Crocheting the head (circular crocheting)

Making a slipknot for the central ring

Making chain stitches in the center

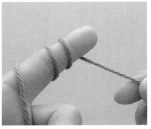

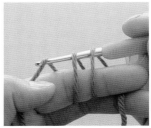

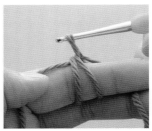

1 Wind the thread twice around the index finger of your left hand.

2 Hold the end of the thread with your index finger and middle finger, and insert the crochet hook into the ring to pull the thread on the left end.

3 Pull the hook through the ring to tighten the ring around your finger.

1 Hook the thread, and pull it through the ring once again.

Making single crochets (first row)

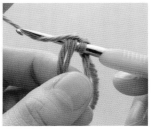

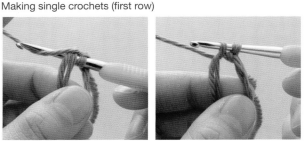

2 The chain stitch is completed in the center.

3 Once the chain stitch is completed in the center, pull your index finger out of the ring, and hook your index finger on the thread you are going to work on. It is easier to crochet if you hold the thread with your ring finger and pinky finger.

1 Insert the crochet hook into the ring, and hook the thread.

2 Insert the thread into the ring, and then pull it out.

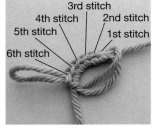

3 Hook the thread once again, and pull out the two stitches together.

4 After pulling out the thread, the single crochet is completed.

5 Repeat steps 1 to 4 five times, and make six stitches with a single crochet.

6 When six stitches are completed, loosen the ring with the hook to pull it out.

Tightening the ring

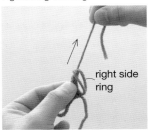

right side ring

right side ring

right side ring

left side ring

right side ring

1 First, pull the end of the thread slightly in the center, and make sure the thread on the right can be tugged.

2 Next, pull the ring tugged on the right side slowly to your side to tighten the ring on the left.

3 The ring is tightened.

Crocheting without starting chains in the center (2nd row)

right side ring

4 After tightening the ring on the left side, pull the end of the thread in the center again to also tighten the ring on the right side.

5 When the ring is tightened, the first row is completed. Now insert the crochet hook.

1 Insert the hook into the first stitch with a single crochet.

2 Hook the thread on the crochet hook and pull it out.

Inserting a row marker ring

Double crochet

3 The thread is pulled out. Hook the thread once again in the same way, and pull the two stitches to make a single crochet.

4 The first stitch in the second row is completed.

Insert a row marker ring into the first stitch of the second row to mark the starting point of the second row. This helps to find the starting point of the circular crocheting, and to make counting stitches and rows easier to do.

Insert the hook into the same stitch, and make one more stitch with a single crochet.

Changing threads

1 Make three stitches with a single crochet in the second row, and stop the hook in the middle of the fourth stitch.

2 Loop the different-colored thread around your finger and hook it. Change threads in the middle of the previous stitch.

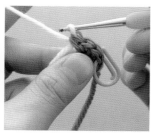

3 Pull the hook with the two stitches hooked together. Now, you have a different-colored stitch.

4 Insert the hook into the next stitch, and pull out the thread, then sew single crochets.

5 Now, one stitch is done with a different-colored thread.

6 As done previously, change the white thread in the middle of the third stitch. Switch to the thread that has been put aside, and pull out the two stitches together.

7 The thread is pulled out. Switch threads and keep on crocheting without cutting the threads when changing their color.

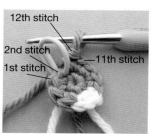

8 When you reach one stitch before the row-counting ring, count the stitches to check if there are twelve stitches.

Replacing the row-counting ring

1 When the first row is done, take out the row-counting ring once, and make one stitch with a single crochet on the stitch that held the ring.

2 Once the stitch is crocheted, insert the row-counting ring into the same stitch. Replace the row-counting ring in each round.

3 Repeat the same steps, and crochet eight rows.

34

Making a single decrease

1 From the 9th row, make a single decrease to the number of stitches. First, insert the hook into a stitch to grab the thread.

2 Pull out the hooked thread.

3 Insert the hook into the next stitch, and grab the thread.

4 Pull out the thread. Here, three stitches are hooked on the crochet hook.

5 Hook the thread over the crochet hook, and pull out the three stitches together.

6 The thread is pulled out. This is a single decrease with a single crochet.

Making a slip stitch to finish

1 To finish with a slip stitch, insert the hook into the next stitch, and pull out the thread.

2 Pull out the other thread hooked on the crochet hook with the thread that was pulled out on the left side.

3 Pull out the thread from the crochet hook, and cut the thread, leaving some extra length.

4 Pull the thread to tighten it.

Making a mouth

Making chain stitches

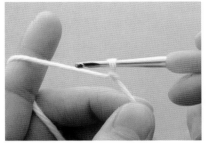

1 Loop the thread on the hook from the rear side to the front, then twist the hook from the front to the rear side.

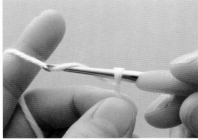

2 Hook the thread with the crochet hook to pull it through. (See page 71.)

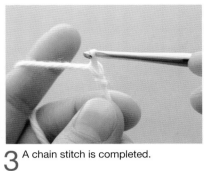

3 A chain stitch is completed.

Making a single crochet (first row)

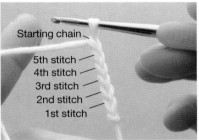

Starting chain
5th stitch
4th stitch
3rd stitch
2nd stitch
1st stitch

4 Repeat steps 2 and 3 to make five chain stitches, then make a starting chain.

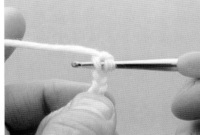

1 Crochet single crochets on the chain stitches. Insert the hook to pull the top of the chain stitch of the 5th stitch on the reverse side.

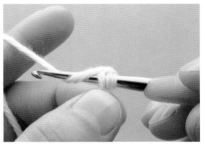

2 Make a single crochet.

3 Insert a row marking ring into the first stitch.

4 Repeating the same steps, crochet four more single crochets into the top of the chain stitches on the reverse side.

5 At the end of the row, crochet two single crochets into one stitch.

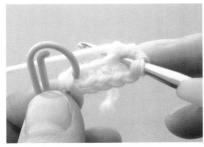

6 Hook a single crochet into the same stitch on the reverse side.

7 Four single crochets are completed.

8 From the next stitch, crochet single crochets on the reverse side by hooking two threads together from the front side of the chain stitch.

Making a slip stitch

9 At the end of the chain stitch, crochet two more stitches into one stitch in the same way as in step 5.

1 Take out the row marking ring, then insert the hook into the first stitch of the first row that had the row marking ring. Pull out the thread over the crochet hook.

2 When the slip stitch is done, the first row is completed.

Sewing the 2nd row

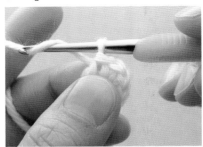

1 First, make a starting chain of the 2nd row.

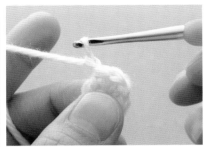

2 Insert the hook into the first stitch with a single crochet, and sew single crochets.

3 Using a single crochet, insert a row-counting ring into the first stitch in the 2nd row.

Making a double decrease

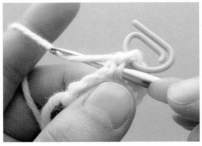

1 First, insert the hook into the first stitch to pull the thread.

2 Pull out the hooked thread

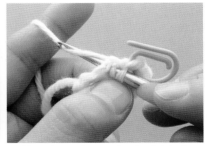

3 Next, insert the crochet hook into the second stitch to pull the thread.

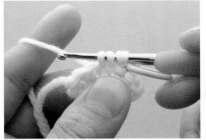

4 Pull out the hooked thread.

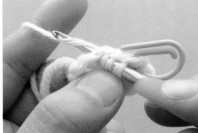

5 Insert the hook into the third stitch to pull the thread.

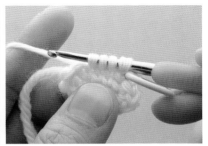

6 Pull out the hooked thread. Now the needle holds four stitches.

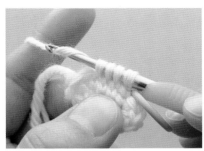

7 Hook the thread on the crochet hook.

8 Pull the four stitches once. The double decrease is completed.

9 Sew five rows to complete the mouth.

Making the body, legs, ears, and tail

As shown on pages 32 and 33, make a slipknot in the center,
crochet single crochets, and make a slip stitch from the
2nd row. Then make a starting chain and crochet single
crochets, as shown on page 37. Finally, make the tail with
circular crocheting in the same manner as the head.

Completed parts

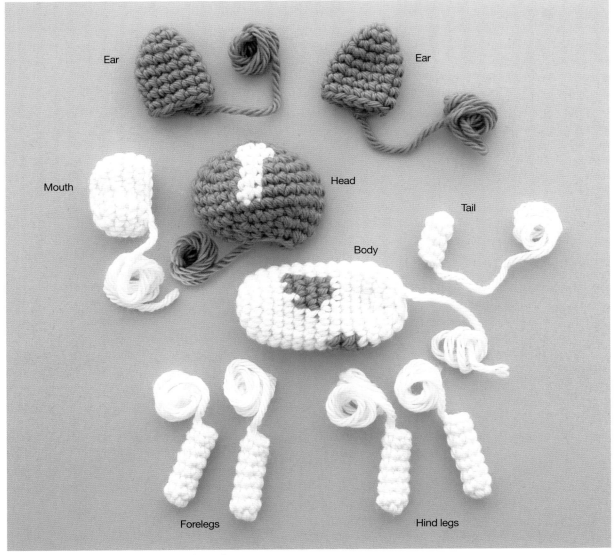

The completed parts are shown in the photo above.
Leave extra thread for the finishing stage.

Stuffing cotton

Stuffing cotton inside the mouth, head, and body

Stuff cotton into the head and the body. Do not stuff cotton inside the ears and tail.

Stuff cotton inside the mouth after attaching the nose to the head. Use a toothpick to stuff cotton into the legs and other tiny parts.

Making the head

Attaching the eyes

1 Insert white thread through the wool needle, and pass the needle from the neck and through the eye. Make a knot at the end of the thread.

2 Pass the needle back through where you pulled it out, and pass it through where the second eye will go.

3 Attach the second eye in the same way, and pull the needle through the rear side. Pass through the thread inside the head a few times, then cut the thread firmly to hide it.

4 The head, including the eyes, is done. To attach eyebrows, continue using the same thread you used for attaching the eyes.

Attaching the nose, mouth, and ears

Attaching the nose

1 Apply glue to the stem of the nose, and push it into the mouth.

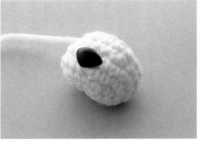

2 Attach the triangular nose with its angle pointing down, and stuff cotton in it.

Attaching the mouth

1 Pass the thread's end through the wool needle. Attach the head.

2 The head, including the mouth, is done.

Attaching the ears

1 Pass the thread's end through the wool needle. Attach the ear to the head from the rear side.

2 After the rear side is attached, pass the needle from the front through the back continuously to attach the ears vertically.

3 To create folded ears, fold one ear and insert the needle into the base of the ear from the rear side. Then pass it through the tip of the ear.

4 Pass the needle from the tip of the ear through the rear side. Repeat this step two or three times.

5 Attach the other ear in the same way to complete the head.

Attaching the head

1 Pass the end of the body's thread through the wool needle, and make running stitches (stitches passing the needle in and out in a straight line) around the edge.

2 After completing one row, pull the thread to tighten, then pass it through the body, and cut the thread.

3 Tighten the end of the head's thread lightly.

4 Pass the end of a leg's thread through the wool needle. Attach the leg to the body.

5 The body is now attached to the head.

Attaching the legs

1 Pass the end of a leg's thread through the wool needle. Attach the leg to the body.

2 After the other leg is attached, pass the same thread through both legs and the body two to three times to affix them. This prevents the legs from spreading apart, and makes the dog stand.

Attaching the tail

1 Attach the tail to complete the work

Making the ears for the Shih Tzu, Toy Poodle, Chihuahua, and Papillon

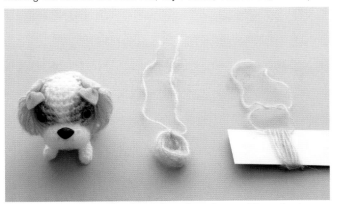

Wind the thread around a piece of cardboard several times to shape it. Tie the top part with another piece of thread, and pull it off the cardboard. Attach it to the head with the same thread that was used to tie it. Refer to the instructions per dog for the width of the cardboard, and the number of times the thread should be wound.

Making the spots for the Dalmatian

Tear a piece of felt wool into pieces of moderate sizes, and softly wad them up with your fingers. Place the pieces on the body, and poke them with a felting needle to twine around the stitches.

Various types and sizes of eyes and noses

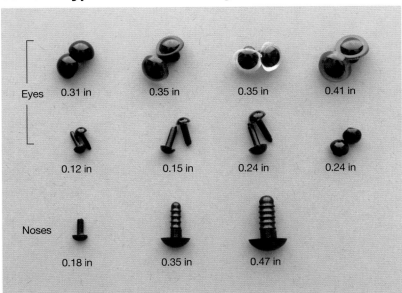

Eyes

0.31 in   0.35 in   0.35 in   0.41 in

0.12 in   0.15 in   0.24 in   0.24 in

Noses

0.18 in   0.35 in   0.47 in

If you wish to outline the rims of the eyes, paint the reverse side of the eyes with a whiteout pen.

There are various types of eyes, such as plastic eyes, plastic sewing buttons, and insertable plastic button eyes. Large 0.41 in eyes are only used for the Chihuahua. For noses, 0.18–0.47 in pegs are used.

Beginners' Guide

Crochet chart symbols

The crocheting method for each dog is accompanied by charts. Refer to the chart symbols below, and start from the first row. The crocheting method is explained in the steps for the Jack Russell Terrier (pages 32–43) in addition to the instructions on page 71.

 Chain stitch

 Single crochet

 Single increase with a single crochet

 Single decrease with a single crochet

 Double decrease with a single crochet

 Slip stitch

Materials

The Jack Russell Terrier shown on page 30 is the standard size. The types of yarns used for each dog are indicated, but you can freely use various yarns in different thicknesses to make dogs in different sizes.

Refer to the dogs shown at the bottom of pages 2 and 3 to see how the different breeds look together. You may choose to make individual dogs smaller or larger to appear as puppies or adult dogs, depending on how you want your family to look.

Tools

Only crochet hooks in different sizes are specified in the step-by-step method for each dog. You will also need a wool needle, scissors, and glue for all projects. See page 31.

Step-by-step method

Refer to the procedures in the step-by-step method for the Jack Russell Terrier. However, you can freely change the order of attaching the ears, legs, tails, and other parts. You can also adjust the position of each part according to your preference, as long as you check the overall balance.

Others

If you are making a seated dog, stuff weights, such as pellets or nuts, inside the buttocks of the dog to keep the dog seated.

Jack Russell Terrier

See page 6.

Both dogs in a standing position and seated position are crocheted in the same way.

Materials (for both types of dogs)

White thread, 0.25 oz
Brown thread, 0.28 oz
Synthetic cotton
Black plastic sewing buttons,
  2 pieces, 0.24 in each
Black nose, 1 piece, 0.47 in

Tool

Crochet hook, No. 4/0

Step-by-step method

1. Crochet each body part.
2. Stuff cotton inside the head, body, and legs.
3. Attach the eyes to the head.
4. Attach the nose to the mouth and stuff cotton in it.
5. Attach the mouth to the head.
6. Attach the ears to the head.
7. Crochet the last row of the body with the remaining thread, tie and knot.
8. Pass the remaining thread through the last row of the head and tighten it lightly, then attach it to the body.
9. Attach the legs and the tail to the body.

Head

c=center

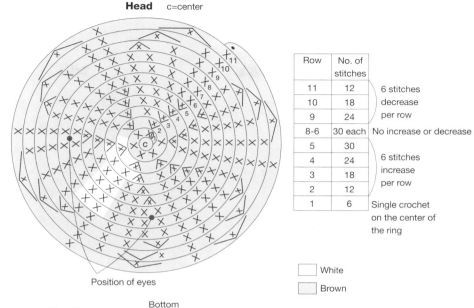

Position of eyes

Row	No. of stitches	
11	12	6 stitches decrease per row
10	18	
9	24	
8-6	30 each	No increase or decrease
5	30	6 stitches increase per row
4	24	
3	18	
2	12	
1	6	Single crochet on the center of the ring

☐ White
▨ Brown

Mouth

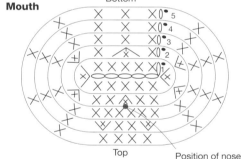

Bottom

Top

Position of nose

Row	No. of stitches	
5	15	No increase or decrease
4	15	2 stitches decrease
3	17	No increase or decrease
2	17	3 stitches increase
1	14	Single crochet around 5 chain stitches

Ears

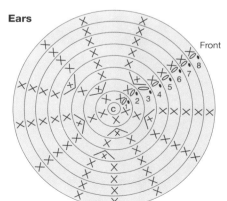

Front

2 pieces

Row	No. of stitches	
8-5	12 each	No increase or decrease
4	12	2 stitches increase
3	10	3 stitches increase
2	7	2 stitches increase
1	5	Single crochet on the center of the ring

Body   c=center

Stomach

15
14
13
12
11
10
9
8
7
6
5
4
3
2
1
c

Back

Row	No. of stitches	
15	6	6 stitches decrease
14	12	4 stitches decrease
13-4	16 each	No increase or decrease
3	16	4 stitches increase
2	12	6 stitches increase
1	6	Single crochet on the center of the ring

☐ White
▨ Brown

Legs

7
6
5
4
3
2
1
c

4 pieces

Row	No. of stitches	
7-2	5 each	No increase or decrease
1	5	Single crochet on the center of the ring

Tail

4
3
2
1
c

Row	No. of stitches	
4-2	5 each	No increase or decrease
1	5	Single crochet on the center of the ring

Attach the tip of the ears to the 7th row of the head. Hide the starting stitch inside.

Position of parts
Standing dog

2nd–6th rows of the head

6th–10th rows of the head

3rd–7th rows of the body

13th and 14th rows of the body

3rd–5th rows of the body

12th–14th rows of the body

Reclining dog

3rd–7th rows of the body

13th and 14th rows of the body

14th row of the body

6th row of the body

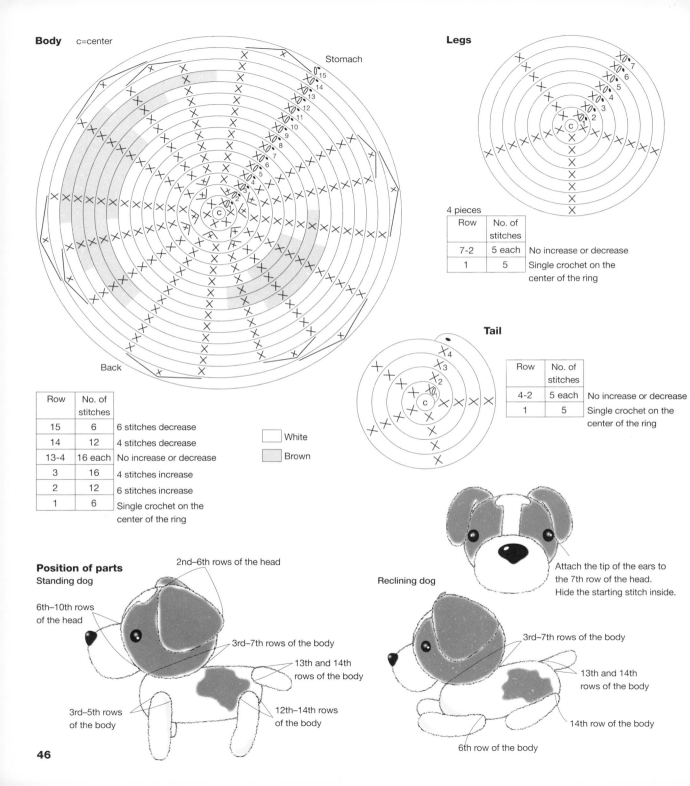

Chihuahua (long coat, cream and white)

See page 4.

The mouth, body, ears, and legs are crocheted in the same way as those of the smooth coat, black and tan Chihuahua. The ears and body are crocheted with beige thread, and the mouth is crocheted with white thread. The legs are crocheted with white thread for two rows, and the rest of the parts are crocheted with beige thread.

Materials

White mohair thread, 0.14 oz
Beige mohair thread, 0.46 oz
Synthetic cotton
Black plastic sewing buttons, 2 pieces, 0.31 in each
Black nose, 1 piece, 0.47 in

Tool

Crochet hook, No. 4/0

Step-by-step method

1. Crochet each body part.
2. Stuff cotton inside the head, body, and legs.
3. Attach the eyes to the head.
4. Attach the nose to the mouth, and stuff cotton in it.
5. Attach the mouth to the head.
6. Attach the ears.
7. Crochet the last row of the body with the remaining thread, tie and knot.
8. Crochet the last row of the head with the remaining thread, tie lightly, and crochet the body.
9. Attach the legs to the body.
10. Make the fur for the ears, chest, and tail by winding thread around a sheet of cardboard.
11. Crochet the fur of the ears and chest.
12. Attach the tail to the body.

Head
c=center

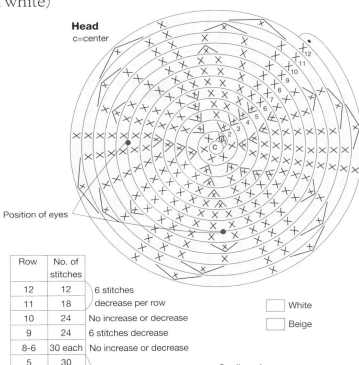

Position of eyes

Row	No. of stitches	
12	12	6 stitches
11	18	decrease per row
10	24	No increase or decrease
9	24	6 stitches decrease
8-6	30 each	No increase or decrease
5	30	
4	24	6 stitches
3	18	increase per row
2	12	
1	6	Single crochet on the center of the ring

White
Beige

Cardboard

0.6 in

To make the fur for the ears, wind a thread three times around a piece of 0.6 in wide cardboard, then pull it out of the cardboard, and tie ten bundles. For the fur of the chest, wind the thread five times in two bundles. For the tail, wind the thread ten times around a piece of 0.78 in cardboard.

Tie

Position of parts

1st row of the ear

3rd row of the ear

5th row of the ear

7th row of the ear

8th row of the head

2 bundles around the neck

7th–10th rows of the head

14th row of the body

14th row of the body

Chihuahua (smooth coat, black and tan)

See page 4.

Embroider the eyebrows with
brown thread.

Materials (for both types of dogs)

Black mohair thread, 0.38 oz
Brown mohair thread, 0.07 oz
White mohair thread, 0.07 oz
Synthetic cotton
Brown plastic eyes, 2 pieces, 0.41 in each
Black nose, 1 piece, 0.47 in

Tool

Crochet hook, No. 4/0

Step-by-step method

1. Crochet each body part.
2. Stuff cotton inside the head, body, and legs.
3. Attach the eyes and the eyebrows to the head.
4. Attach the nose to the mouth, and stuff cotton
in it.
5. Attach the mouth to the head.
6. Attach the ears to the head.
7. Crochet the last row of the body with the
remaining thread, tie and knot.
8. Crochet the last row of the head with the
remaining thread, tie lightly, and crochet
the body.
9. Attach the legs and the tail to the body.

Head c=center

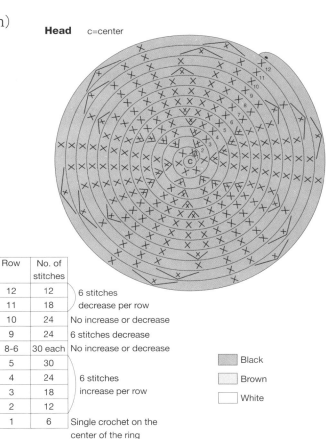

Row	No. of stitches	
12	12	6 stitches decrease per row
11	18	
10	24	No increase or decrease
9	24	6 stitches decrease
8-6	30 each	No increase or decrease
5	30	6 stitches increase per row
4	24	
3	18	
2	12	
1	6	Single crochet on the center of the ring

	Black
	Brown
	White

Ears

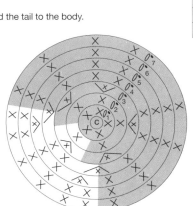

2 pieces

Row	No. of stitches	
7-6	14 each	No increase or decrease
5	14	2 stitches increase
4	12	2 stitches increase
3	10	5 stitches increase
2	5	No increase or decrease
1	5	Single crochet on the center of the ring

Mouth

Bottom

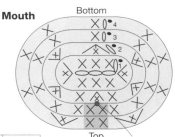

Top

Position of nose

Row	No. of stitches	
4	11	2 stitches decrease
3	13	No increase or decrease
2	13	3 stitches increase
1	10	Single crochet around 3 chain stitches

Body

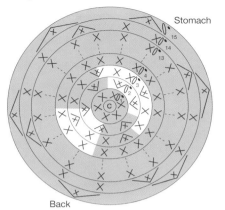

Stomach

Back

Row	No. of stitches	
15	6	6 stitches decrease
14	12	4 stitches decrease
13-4	16 each	No increase or decrease
3	16	4 stitches increase
2	12	6 stitches increase
1	6	Single crochet on the center of the ring

Legs

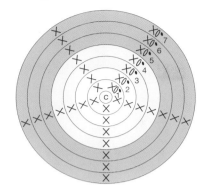

4 pieces

Row	No. of stitches	
7-2	5 each	No increase or decrease
1	5	Single crochet on the center of the ring

Tail

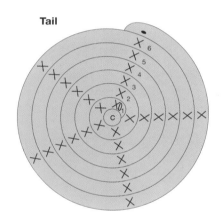

Row	No. of stitches	
6-2	5 each	No increase or decrease
1	5	Single crochet on the center of the ring

Position of parts

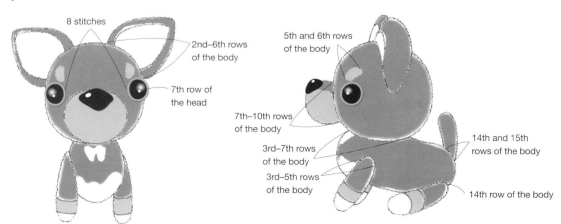

8 stitches

2nd–6th rows of the body

7th row of the head

5th and 6th rows of the body

7th–10th rows of the body

3rd–7th rows of the body

3rd–5th rows of the body

14th and 15th rows of the body

14th row of the body

Toy Poodle   See page 8.

Crochet the ears by winding the thread thirty times around a sheet of 1.57 in wide cardboard, as shown on pages 43 and 47.

Materials

[White]
White mohair thread, 0.42 oz

[Black]
Black mohair thread, 0.42 oz

[Apricot]
Brown mohair thread, 0.42 oz
Synthetic cotton
Black plastic sewing buttons, 2 pieces,
   0.24 in for each color
Black nose, 1 piece, 0.47 in for each color

Tool

Crochet hook, No. 4/0

Step-by-step method

[Seated dog]
1. Crochet each body part. Turn the reverse side of the stitches for each part.
2. Stuff cotton inside the head, body, and legs.
3. Attach the eyes to the head.
4. Attach the nose to the mouth, and stuff cotton in it.
5. Attach the mouth to the head.
6. Attach the body to the head.
7. Attach the legs and the tail to the body.
8. Wind wool around a sheet of cardboard to make the ears.
9. Attach the ears to the head.

[Reclining Toy Poodle]
1–5. Same as above
6. Crochet the last row of the body with the remaining thread, tie and knot.
7. Crochet the last row of the head with the remaining thread, tie lightly, and crochet the body.
8–10. Same as steps 7–9 of the seated dog

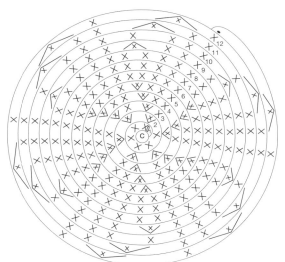

Bottom

Top   Position of nose

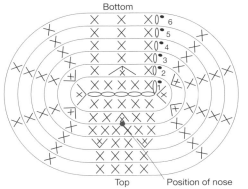

Front

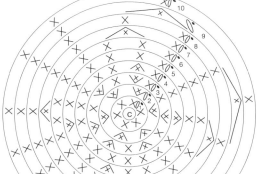

Head
c=center

Row	No. of stitches	
12	12	6 stitches decrease per row
11	18	
10	24	No increase or decrease
9	24	6 stitches decrease
8-6	30 each	No increase or decrease
5	30	
4	24	6 stitches increase per row
3	18	
2	12	
1	6	Single crochet on the center of the ring

Mouth

Row	No. of stitches	
6-5	15 each	No increase or decrease
4	15	2 stitches decrease
3	17	No increase or decrease
2	17	3 stitches increase
1	14	Single crochet around 5 chain stitches

Body of seated dog

Row	No. of stitches	
10	12	No increase or decrease
9	12	2 stitches decrease
8	14	No increase or decrease
7	14	4 stitches decrease
6	18	No increase or decrease
5	18	2 stitches increase
4	16	2 stitches decrease
3	18	6 stitches increase per row
2	12	
1	6	Single crochet on the center of the ring

Body of reclining and seated dog

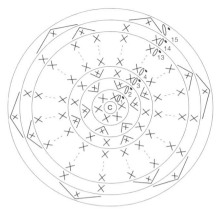

Row	No. of stitches	
15	6	6 stitches decrease
14	12	4 stitches decrease
13-4	16 each	No increase or decrease
3	16	4 stitches increase
2	12	6 stitches increase
1	6	Single crochet on the center of the ring

Legs of seated dog

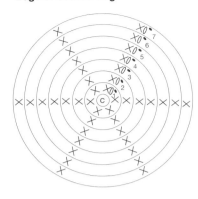

Forelegs, 2 pieces

Row	No. of stitches	
7-2	6 each	No increase or decrease
1	6	Single crochet on the center of the ring

Crochet 6 rows to make 1 pair of hind legs.

Legs of reclining and standing dog

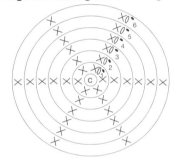

4 pieces

Row	No. of stitches	
6-2	6 each	No increase or decrease
1	6	Single crochet on the center of the ring

Position of parts

7th row of the head

Seated dog

5th row of the head

8 stitches

9th row of the body

2nd–4th rows of the body

Reclining dog

13th and 14th rows of the body

14th row of the body

3rd–7th rows of the body

6th row of the body

Tail

Row	No. of stitches	
4-2	6 each	No increase or decrease
1	6	Single crochet on the center of the ring

Standing dog

13th and 14th rows of the body

7th–11th rows of the head

12th–14th rows of the body

3rd–5th rows of the body

Shih Tzu   See page 10.

The legs are crocheted in the same way as the Jack Russell Terrier—seven rows for the front legs of the seated dog, six rows for the hind legs of the seated dog, and all the rows for the legs of the reclining dog. The ears are crocheted by winding the thread 15 times around a sheet of 1.57 in wide cardboard, as shown on pages 43 and 47. The tail is crocheted by winding the thread 10 times around a sheet of 1.18 in wide cardboard.

Materials (for both types of dogs)
[White and silver]
White mohair thread, 0.25 oz
Gray mohair thread, 0.25 oz
Pink felt, 2 sheets, 0.6 in x 0.78 in each
Synthetic cotton
Brown plastic sewing buttons, 2 pieces, 0.35 in each
Black nose, 1 piece, 0.47 in

[White and gold]
White mohair thread, 0.25 oz
Brown mohair thread, 0.25 oz
Red felt, 2 sheets, 0.6 in x 0.78 in each
The rest of the materials are the same as those for the white and silver dog.

Tool
Crochet hook, No. 4/0

Step-by-step method
[Reclining Shih Tzu]
1. Crochet each body part.
2. Stuff cotton inside the head, body, and legs.
3. Attach the eyes to the head.
4. Attach the nose to the mouth, with its seam in front, and stuff cotton in it.
5. Attach the mouth to the head.
6. Crochet the last row of the body with the remaining thread, tie and knot.
7. Pass the remaining thread through the last row of the head and tighten it lightly, then, attach it to the body.
8. Attach the legs to the body.
9. Wind wool around a sheet of cardboard to make the ears and the tail.
10. Attach the ears to the head.
11. Attach the tail to the body, and glue the base of the tail by twisting it.
12. Make ribbons, and glue them on the ears.

[Seated Shih Tzu]
1–5. Same steps as above.
6. Attach the body to the head.
7–11. Same as steps 8–12 above

Head   c=center

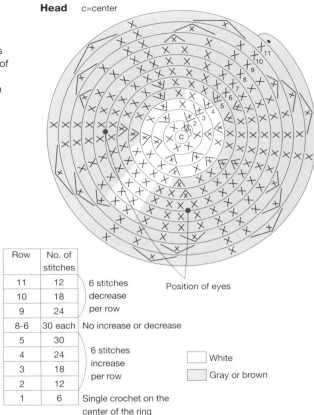

Position of eyes

Row	No. of stitches	
11	12	6 stitches decrease per row
10	18	
9	24	
8-6	30 each	No increase or decrease
5	30	
4	24	6 stitches increase per row
3	18	
2	12	
1	6	Single crochet on the center of the ring

□ White
▨ Gray or brown

Mouth   Bottom

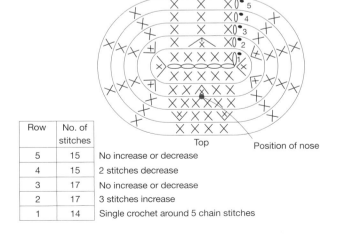

Top

Position of nose

Row	No. of stitches	
5	15	No increase or decrease
4	15	2 stitches decrease
3	17	No increase or decrease
2	17	3 stitches increase
1	14	Single crochet around 5 chain stitches

Body of reclining Shih Tzu

Stomach

Back

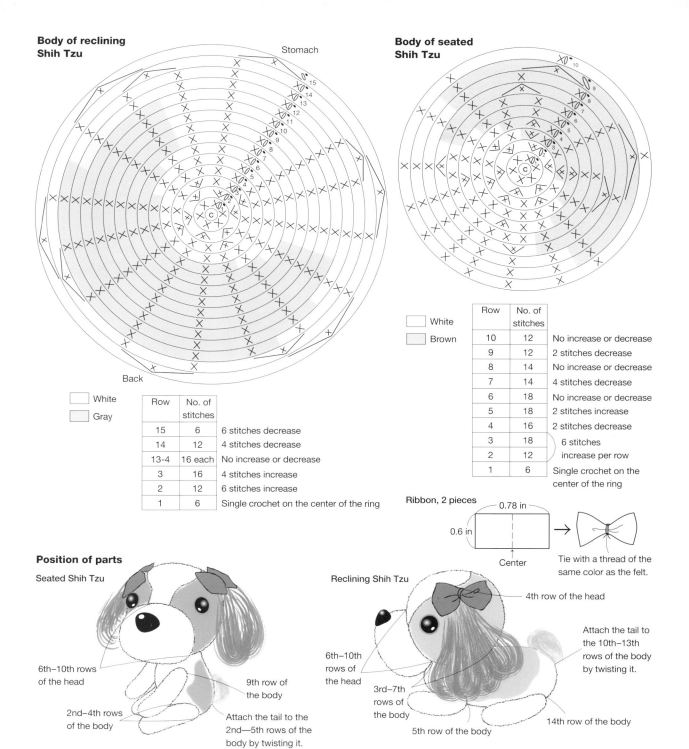

	White
	Gray

Row	No. of stitches	
15	6	6 stitches decrease
14	12	4 stitches decrease
13-4	16 each	No increase or decrease
3	16	4 stitches increase
2	12	6 stitches increase
1	6	Single crochet on the center of the ring

Body of seated Shih Tzu

	White
	Brown

Row	No. of stitches	
10	12	No increase or decrease
9	12	2 stitches decrease
8	14	No increase or decrease
7	14	4 stitches decrease
6	18	No increase or decrease
5	18	2 stitches increase
4	16	2 stitches decrease
3	18	6 stitches increase per row
2	12	
1	6	Single crochet on the center of the ring

Ribbon, 2 pieces

0.78 in

0.6 in

Center

Tie with a thread of the same color as the felt.

Position of parts

Seated Shih Tzu

6th–10th rows of the head

2nd–4th rows of the body

9th row of the body

Attach the tail to the 2nd—5th rows of the body by twisting it.

Reclining Shih Tzu

4th row of the head

6th–10th rows of the head

3rd–7th rows of the body

5th row of the body

Attach the tail to the 10th–13th rows of the body by twisting it.

14th row of the body

Dalmatian   See page 12.

The body is crocheted in the same way as the Toy Poodle. The ears are folded in half, crocheted, and attached to the head.

Materials (for both types of dogs)

[White Mother Dalmatian]
White thread, 0.42 oz

[Mother Dalmatian with black ears]
White thread, 0.38 oz
Black thread, 0.07 oz
Black wool felt
Synthetic cotton
Black plastic sewing buttons, 2 pieces, 0.24 in each
Black nose, 1 piece, 0.47 in

[White Dalmatian puppy]
White thread, 0.32 oz

[Dalmatian puppy with black ears]
White thread, 0.28 oz
Black thread, 0.07 oz
Black wool felt
Synthetic cotton
Black eyes, 2 pieces, 0.15 in each
Black nose, 1 piece, 0.35 in

Tool

[Mother Dalmatian] Crochet needle No. 4/0
[Dalmatian puppy] Crochet needle No. 3/0
Felting needle

Step-by-step method

[Sitting Dalmatian]
1. Crochet each body part.
2. Stuff cotton inside the head, body, and legs.
3. Attach the eyes to the head.
4. Attach the nose to the mouth, and stuff cotton in it.
5. Attach the mouth to the head.
6. Fold the ears in half, and crochet each of them with the remaining thread, then attach them to the head.
7. Attach the body to the head.
8. Attach the legs and the tail to the body.
9. Get some wool, and poke it randomly around the body with a felting needle.

[Reclining, standing, or sleeping Dalmatian]
1–6. Same steps as above
7. Crochet the last row of the body with the remaining thread, tie and knot.
8. Pass the remaining thread through the last row of the head and tighten it lightly, then attach it to the body.
9–10. Same as steps 8 and 9 above

Head   c=center

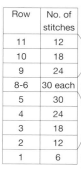

Row	No. of stitches	
11	12	6 stitches decrease per row
10	18	
9	24	
8-6	30 each	No increase or decrease
5	30	6 stitches increase per row
4	24	
3	18	
2	12	
1	6	Single crochet on the center of the ring

Mouth

Row	No. of stitches	
5	15	No increase or decrease
4	15	2 stitches decrease
3	17	No increase or decrease
2	17	3 stitches increase
1	14	Single crochet around 5 chain stitches

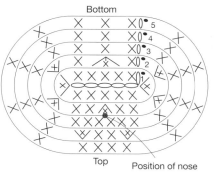

Bottom

Top

Position of nose

Ears

2 pieces

Row	No. of stitches	
4	14	2 stitches decrease
3	16	6 stitches increase
2	10	4 stitches increase
1	6	Single crochet on the center of the ring

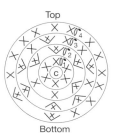

Top

Bottom

Tail

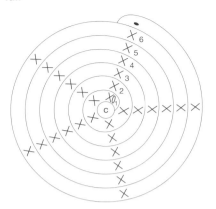

Legs

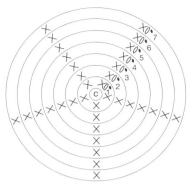

Row	No. of stitches	
6-2	5 each	No increase or decrease
1	5	Single crochet on the center of the ring

Forelegs of seated and sleeping Dalmatians

Row	No. of stitches	
7-2	5 each	No increase or decrease
1	5	Single crochet on the center of the ring

Other legs

Row	No. of stitches	
6-2	5 each	No increase or decrease
1	5	Single crochet on the center of the ring

Position of parts

Standing Dalmatian

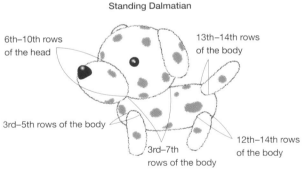

6th–10th rows of the head

13th–14th rows of the body

3rd–5th rows of the body

3rd–7th rows of the body

12th–14th rows of the body

Seated Dalmatian

9th row of the body

Attach the hind legs and the tail to the 3rd and 4th rows of the body.

Sleeping Dalmatian

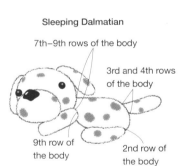

7th–9th rows of the body

3rd and 4th rows of the body

9th row of the body

2nd row of the body

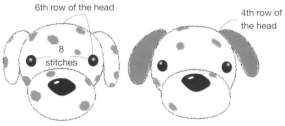

6th row of the head

8 stitches

4th row of the head

Reclining Dalmatian

6th row of the body

14th row of the body

Papillon   See page 14.

To make the fur of the ears, wind the thread three times around a piece of 1.38 in wide cardboard, and make ten bundles. To make the fur of the chest, wind the thread five times, and make three bundles. To make the tail, wind the thread ten times around a piece of 0.78 in wide cardboard. The method for attaching the fur of the ears and tail is the same method as that for the long-coat Chihuahua.

Materials
[White and brown]
White mohair thread, 0.28 oz
Brown mohair thread, 0.28 oz
Synthetic cotton
Black plastic sewing buttons, 2 pieces, 0.24 in each
Black nose, 1 piece, 0.47 in

[White and black]
White mohair thread, 0.28 oz
Black mohair thread, 0.28 oz
Synthetic cotton
Brown plastic eyes, 2 pieces, 0.24 in each
Black nose, 1 piece, 0.47 in

Tool
Crochet hook, No. 4/0

Step-by-step method (for both colors)
1. Crochet each body part.
2. Stuff cotton inside the head, body, and legs.
3. Attach the eyes to the head.
4. Attach the nose to the mouth, and stuff cotton in it.
5. Attach the mouth to the head.
6. Attach the ears.
7. Crochet the last row of the body with the remaining thread, tie and knot.
8. Pass the remaining thread through the last row of the head and tighten it lightly, then, attach it to the body.
9. Attach the legs to the body.
10. Wind wool around a sheet of cardboard to make the tail and the fur of the ears and chest.
11. Crochet to attach the furs of the ears and chest.
12. Attach the tail to the body.
13. Trim two bundles of furs above the ears and the fur of the chest.

Head   c=center

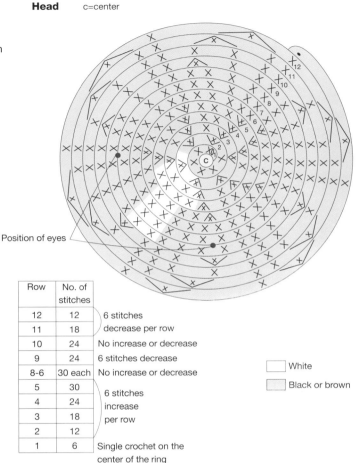

Position of eyes

Row	No. of stitches	
12	12	6 stitches decrease per row
11	18	
10	24	No increase or decrease
9	24	6 stitches decrease
8-6	30 each	No increase or decrease
5	30	6 stitches increase per row
4	24	
3	18	
2	12	
1	6	Single crochet on the center of the ring

☐ White
▨ Black or brown

Mouth

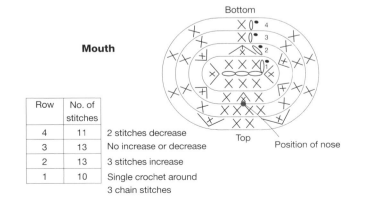

Bottom

Top

Position of nose

Row	No. of stitches	
4	11	2 stitches decrease
3	13	No increase or decrease
2	13	3 stitches increase
1	10	Single crochet around 3 chain stitches

Body

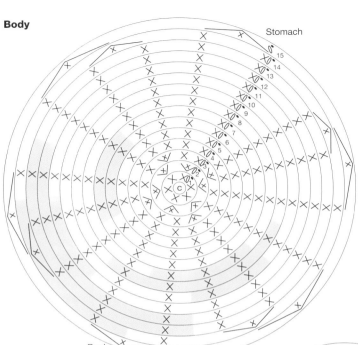

Stomach

Back

Row	No. of stitches	
15	6	6 stitches decrease
14	12	4 stitches decrease
13-4	16 each	No increase or decrease
3	16	4 stitches increase
2	12	6 stitches increase
1	6	Single crochet on the center of the ring

Ears

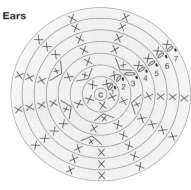

2 pieces

Row	No. of stitches	
7-5	12 each	No increase or decrease
4	12	2 stitches increase
3	10	3 stitches increase
2	7	2 stitches increase
1	5	Single crochet on the center of the ring

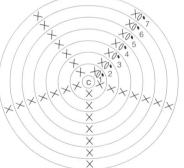

Legs

4 pieces

Row	No. of stitches	
7-2	5 each	No increase or decrease
1	5	Single crochet on the center of the ring

Position of parts

2nd–5th rows of the head

Trim the fur diagonally.

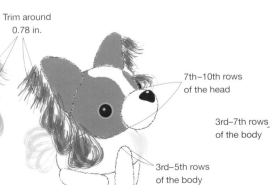

Trim around 0.78 in.

7th–10th rows of the head

3rd–5th rows of the body

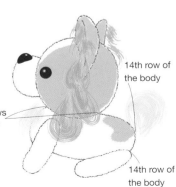

14th row of the body

3rd–7th rows of the body

14th row of the body

Boston Terrier　　See page 16.

The mouth is crocheted in the same way as that of the Jack Russell Terrier.

Materials (same for both types)
Black thread, 0.32 oz
White thread, 0.18 oz
Pink thread, 0.07 oz
Synthetic cotton
Clear plastic eyes, 2 pieces, 0.35 in each
Black nose, 1 piece, 0.47 in

Tool
Crochet hook, No. 4/0

Step-by-step method
[Seated Boston Terrier]
1. Crochet each body part.
2. Stuff cotton inside the head, body, and legs.
3. Attach the eyes to the head. Paint the reverse side of the eyes with correction fluid.
4. Attach the nose to the mouth, with its seam in front, and stuff cotton in it.
5. Attach the mouth to the head.
6. Attach the ears to the head.
7. Attach the body to the head.
8. Attach the legs and the tail to the body.

[Reclining Boston Terrier]
1–6. Same steps as above
7. Pass the remaining thread through the last row of the head and tighten it lightly, then, attach it to the body.
8. Attach the legs and the tail to the body.

Head　　c=center

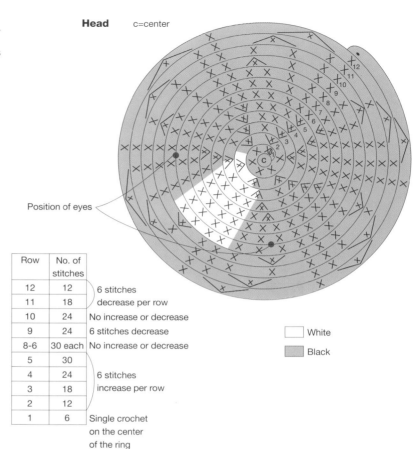

Position of eyes

Row	No. of stitches	
12	12	6 stitches decrease per row
11	18	
10	24	No increase or decrease
9	24	6 stitches decrease
8-6	30 each	No increase or decrease
5	30	
4	24	6 stitches increase per row
3	18	
2	12	
1	6	Single crochet on the center of the ring

☐ White
▨ Black

Body

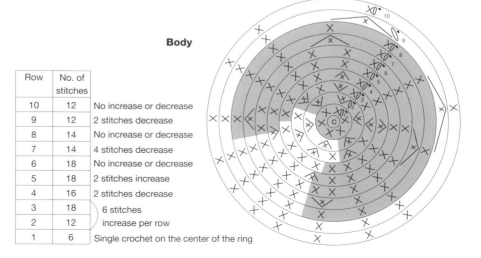

Row	No. of stitches	
10	12	No increase or decrease
9	12	2 stitches decrease
8	14	No increase or decrease
7	14	4 stitches decrease
6	18	No increase or decrease
5	18	2 stitches increase
4	16	2 stitches decrease
3	18	6 stitches increase per row
2	12	
1	6	Single crochet on the center of the ring

Legs

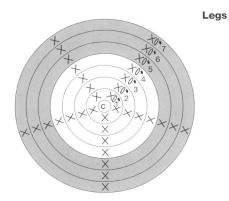 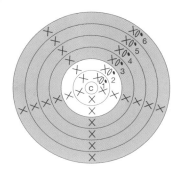

Ears

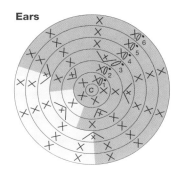

Forelegs, 2 pieces

Row	No. of stitches	
7-2	5 each	No increase or decrease
1	5	Single crochet on the center of the ring

Hind legs, 2 pieces

Row	No. of stitches	
6-2	5 each	No increase or decrease
1	5	Single crochet on the center of the ring

2 pieces

Row	No. of stitches	
6-5	12 each	No increase or decrease
4	12	2 stitches increase
3	10	3 stitches increase
2	7	2 stitches increase
1	5	Single crochet on the center of the ring

White   Pink   Black

Tail

Row	No. of stitches	
1	5	Single crochet on the center of the ring

Position of parts

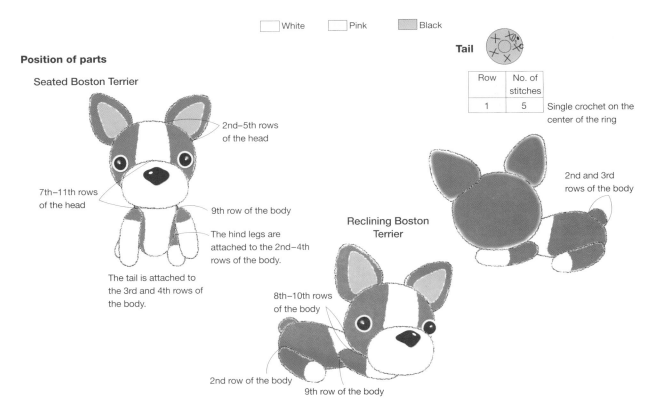

Seated Boston Terrier

2nd–5th rows of the head

7th–11th rows of the head

9th row of the body

The hind legs are attached to the 2nd–4th rows of the body.

The tail is attached to the 3rd and 4th rows of the body.

Reclining Boston Terrier

8th–10th rows of the body

2nd and 3rd rows of the body

2nd row of the body

9th row of the body

Bernese Mountain Dog   See page 18.

The legs are crocheted in six rows in the same way as those of the black and tan Chihuahua on pages 48–49.

Materials (same for all three types)
Black wool, 0.64 oz
White wool, 0.18 oz
Brown wool, 0.11 oz
Synthetic cotton
Brown plastic eyes, 2 pieces, 0.35 in each
Black nose, 1 piece, 0.47 in

Tool
Crochet hook, No. 4/0

Step-by-step method
[Reclining and standing dogs]
1. Crochet each body part.
2. Stuff cotton inside the head, body, and legs.
3. Attach the eyes and eyebrows to the head.
4. Attach the nose to the mouth, and stuff cotton in it.
5. Attach the mouth to the head.
6. Fold the ears in half, and crochet each of them with the remaining thread, then attach them to the head.
7. Crochet the last row of the body with the remaining thread, tie and knot.
8. Pass the remaining thread through the last row of the head and tighten it lightly, then attach it to the body.
9. Attach the legs and the tail to the body.

[Seated dog]
1–6. Same steps as above
7. Attach the body to the head.
8. Attach the legs and the tail to the body.

Head   c=center

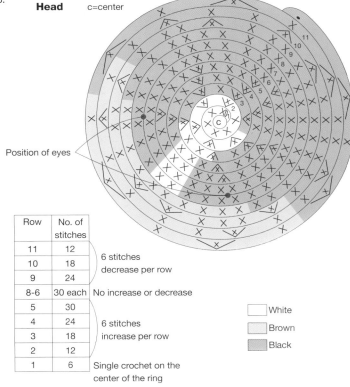

Position of eyes

Row	No. of stitches	
11	12	6 stitches decrease per row
10	18	
9	24	
8-6	30 each	No increase or decrease
5	30	
4	24	6 stitches increase per row
3	18	
2	12	
1	6	Single crochet on the center of the ring

White
Brown
Black

Ears

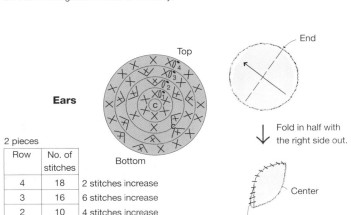

Top

Bottom

End

Fold in half with the right side out.

Center

Close with the remaining thread.

2 pieces

Row	No. of stitches	
4	18	2 stitches increase
3	16	6 stitches increase
2	10	4 stitches increase
1	6	Single crochet on the center of the ring

Mouth

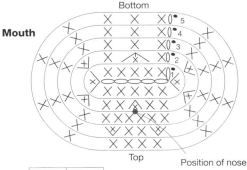

Bottom

Top

Position of nose

Row	No. of stitches	
5	15	No increase or decrease
4	15	2 stitches decrease
3	17	No increase or decrease
2	17	3 stitches increase
1	14	Single crochet around 5 chain stitches

Body of seated dog

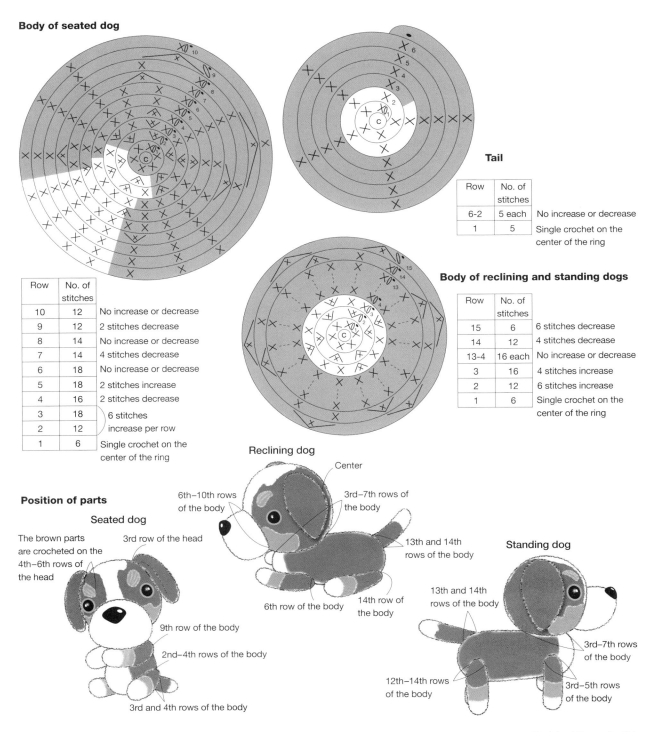

Tail

Body of reclining and standing dogs

Row	No. of stitches	
10	12	No increase or decrease
9	12	2 stitches decrease
8	14	No increase or decrease
7	14	4 stitches decrease
6	18	No increase or decrease
5	18	2 stitches increase
4	16	2 stitches decrease
3	18	6 stitches increase per row
2	12	
1	6	Single crochet on the center of the ring

Tail

Row	No. of stitches	
6-2	5 each	No increase or decrease
1	5	Single crochet on the center of the ring

Body of reclining and standing dogs

Row	No. of stitches	
15	6	6 stitches decrease
14	12	4 stitches decrease
13-4	16 each	No increase or decrease
3	16	4 stitches increase
2	12	6 stitches increase
1	6	Single crochet on the center of the ring

Position of parts

Seated dog

The brown parts are crocheted on the 4th–6th rows of the head

3rd row of the head

9th row of the body

2nd–4th rows of the body

3rd and 4th rows of the body

Reclining dog

Center

6th–10th rows of the body

3rd–7th rows of the body

13th and 14th rows of the body

6th row of the body

14th row of the body

Standing dog

13th and 14th rows of the body

3rd–7th rows of the body

12th–14th rows of the body

3rd–5th rows of the body

Hokkaido Dog   See page 20.

The body is crocheted in the same way as the reclining Toy Poodle on pages 50–51. The tail is crocheted in a single color, like the Japanese Shiba dog on pages 64–65.

Materials (same for both types)
White bulky wool blend thread, 0.78 oz
Red thread
Synthetic cotton
Black plastic sewing buttons, 2 pieces, 0.24 in each
Black nose, 1 piece, 0.47 in

Tool
Crochet hook, No. 4/0

Step-by-step method
[Standing dog]
1. Crochet each body part.
2. Stuff cotton inside the head, body, and legs.
3. Attach the eyes to the head.
4. Attach the nose to the mouth, and stuff cotton in it.
5. Attach the mouth to the head.
6. Attach the ears.
7. Crochet the last row of the body with the remaining thread, tie and knot.
8. Pass the remaining thread through the last row of the head and tighten it lightly, then, attach it to the body.
9. Attach the legs and the tail to the body.
10. Put a collar around the neck

[Seated dog]
1–6. Same steps as above
7. Attach the body to the head.
8–9. Same as steps 9 and 10 above

Head   c=center

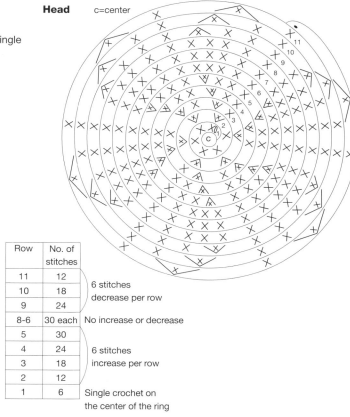

Row	No. of stitches	
11	12	6 stitches decrease per row
10	18	
9	24	
8-6	30 each	No increase or decrease
5	30	
4	24	6 stitches increase per row
3	18	
2	12	
1	6	Single crochet on the center of the ring

Mouth

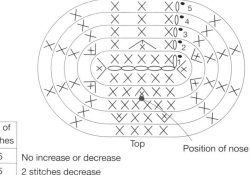

Bottom

Top

Position of nose

Row	No. of stitches	
5	15	No increase or decrease
4	15	2 stitches decrease
3	17	No increase or decrease
2	17	3 stitches increase
1	14	Single crochet around 5 chain stitches

Legs of seated dog

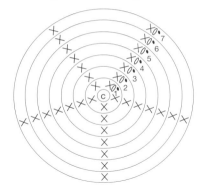

Row	No. of stitches	
7-2	5 each	No increase or decrease
1	5	Single crochet on the center of the ring

Crochet 7 rows for the pair of forelegs, and 6 rows for the pair of hind legs.

Legs of standing dog

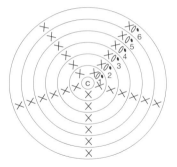

4 pieces

Row	No. of stitches	
6-2	5 each	No increase or decrease
1	5	Single crochet on the center of the ring

Ears

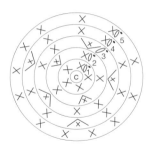

2 pieces

Row	No. of stitches	
5	12	No increase or decrease
4	12	2 stitches increase
3	10	3 stitches increase
2	7	2 stitches increase
1	5	Single crochet on the center of the ring

Collar (red)

Crochet chain stitches to match the girth of the neck, and make slip stitches on the chain stitches.

Position of parts

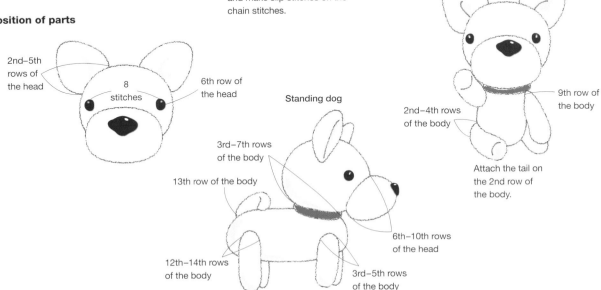

2nd–5th rows of the head

8 stitches

6th row of the head

Standing dog

3rd–7th rows of the body

13th row of the body

12th–14th rows of the body

3rd–5th rows of the body

6th–10th rows of the head

Seated dog

2nd–4th rows of the body

9th row of the body

Attach the tail on the 2nd row of the body.

Japanese Shiba See page 22.

For the puppy, use brown thread under the eyes.

Materials

[Mother Shiba dog]
Black bulky wool blend thread, 0.64 oz
White bulky wool blend thread, 0.28 oz
Brown bulky wool blend thread, 0.07 oz
Synthetic cotton
Brown plastic eyes, 2 pieces, 0.35 in each
Black nose, 1 piece, 0.47 in

[Puppy]
Black light thread, 0.25 oz
White light thread, 0.11 oz
Brown light thread, 0.14 oz
Synthetic cotton
Brown plastic eyes, 2 pieces, 0.24 in each
Black nose, 1 piece, 0.35 in

Tool

[Mother]
Crochet hook No. 4/0
[Puppy]
Crochet hook No. 3/0

Step-by-step method (same for both types)

1. Crochet each body part.
2. Stuff cotton inside the head, body, and legs.
3. Attach the eyes and the eyebrows to the head.
4. Attach the nose to the mouth, and stuff cotton in it.
5. Attach the mouth to the head.
6. Attach the ears.
7. Crochet the last row of the body with the remaining thread, tie and knot.
8. Pass the remaining thread through the last row of the head and tighten it lightly, then attach it to the body.
9. Attach the legs and the tail to the body.

Head c=center

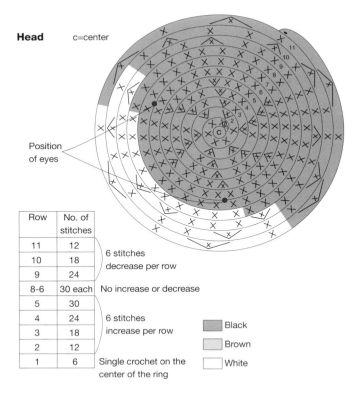

Position of eyes

Row	No. of stitches	
11	12	6 stitches decrease per row
10	18	
9	24	
8-6	30 each	No increase or decrease
5	30	
4	24	6 stitches increase per row
3	18	
2	12	
1	6	Single crochet on the center of the ring

■ Black
▨ Brown
□ White

Mouth

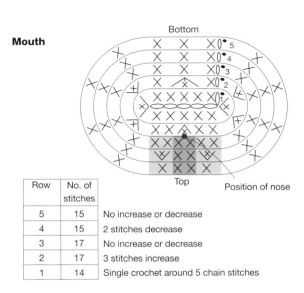

Bottom

Top

Position of nose

Row	No. of stitches	
5	15	No increase or decrease
4	15	2 stitches decrease
3	17	No increase or decrease
2	17	3 stitches increase
1	14	Single crochet around 5 chain stitches

Body

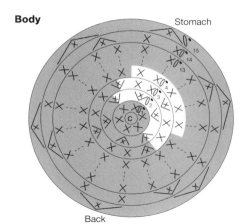

Stomach

Back

Row	No. of stitches	
15	6	6 stitches decrease
14	12	4 stitches decrease
13-4	16 each	No increase or decrease
3	16	4 stitches increase
2	12	6 stitches increase
1	6	Single crochet on the center of the ring

Legs

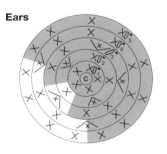

Forelegs, 2 pieces

Row	No. of stitches	
7-2	5 each	No increase or decrease
1	5	Single crochet on the center of the ring

Hind legs, 2 pieces

Row	No. of stitches	
6-2	5 each	No increase or decrease
1	5	Single crochet on the center of the ring

Ears

2 pieces

Row	No. of stitches	
5	12	No increase or decrease
4	12	2 stitches increase
3	10	3 stitches increase
2	7	2 stitches increase
1	5	Single crochet on the center of the ring

Tail

X X X X X X → 2
X X X X X X ←1

Row	No. of stitches	
2	5	Single crochet
1	6	Single crochet around 6 chain stitches

Position of parts

2nd–5th rows of the head

Crochet with brown thread on the 4th and 5th rows of the head.

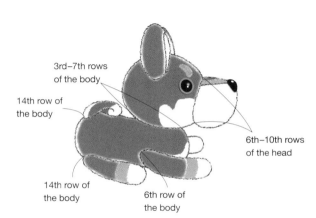

3rd–7th rows of the body

14th row of the body

6th–10th rows of the head

14th row of the body

6th row of the body

Bull Terrier

See page 24.

Materials (same for both types)
White thread, 0.64 oz
Black thread, 0.04 oz
Pink thread, 0.07 oz
Synthetic cotton
Clear plastic eyes, 2 pieces, 0.35 in each
Black nose, 1 piece, 0.47 in

Tool
Crochet hook No. 4/0

Step-by-step method (same for both types)
1. Crochet each body part.
2. Stuff cotton inside the head, body, and legs.
3. Attach the eyes to the head, and paint the reverse side of the eyes with correction fluid.
4. Attach the nose to the mouth, and stuff cotton in it.
5. Attach the mouth to the head.
6. Attach the ears.
7. Crochet the last row of the body with the remaining thread, tie and knot.
8. Pass the remaining thread through the last row of the head and tighten it lightly, then attach it to the body.
9. Attach the legs and the tail to the body.

Head c=center

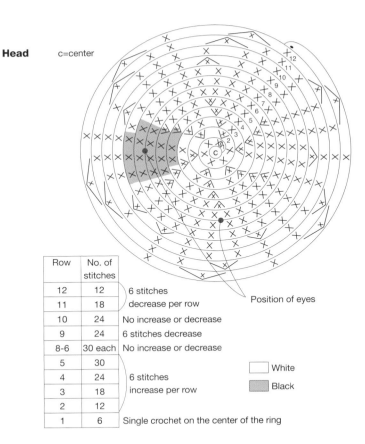

Position of eyes

Row	No. of stitches	
12	12	6 stitches decrease per row
11	18	
10	24	No increase or decrease
9	24	6 stitches decrease
8-6	30 each	No increase or decrease
5	30	
4	24	6 stitches increase per row
3	18	
2	12	
1	6	Single crochet on the center of the ring

☐ White
▨ Black

Legs

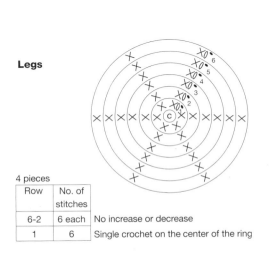

4 pieces

Row	No. of stitches	
6-2	6 each	No increase or decrease
1	6	Single crochet on the center of the ring

Mouth

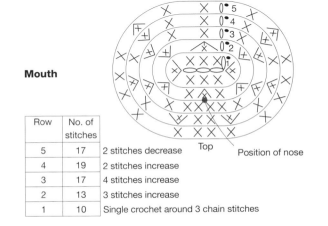

Bottom

Top

Position of nose

Row	No. of stitches	
5	17	2 stitches decrease
4	19	2 stitches increase
3	17	4 stitches increase
2	13	3 stitches increase
1	10	Single crochet around 3 chain stitches

Body

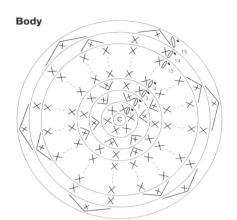

Row	No. of stitches	
15	6	6 stitches decrease
14	12	4 stitches decrease
13-4	16 each	No increase or decrease
3	16	4 stitches increase
2	12	6 stitches increase
1	6	Single crochet on the center of the ring

Ears

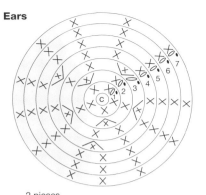

2 pieces

Row	No. of stitches	
7-5	12 each	No increase or decrease
4	12	2 stitches increase
3	10	3 stitches increase
2	7	2 stitches increase
1	5	Single crochet on the center of the ring

☐ White
☐ Pink

Tail

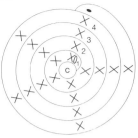

Row	No. of stitches	
4-2	5 each	No increase or decrease
1	5	Single crochet on the center of the ring

2nd–6th rows of the head

6th–11th rows of the head

12th–14th rows of the body

Position of parts

Bull Terrier lying on its back

3rd–5th rows of the body

13th and 14th rows of the body

Attach the head to the 1st and 2nd rows of the body.

Bull Terrier lying on its stomach

3rd–6th rows of the body

13th and 14th rows of the body

14th row of the body

6th row of the body

Tail of cellular phone strap

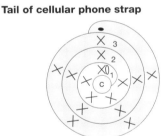

Row	No. of stitches	
3-2	5 each	No increase or decrease
1	5	Single crochet on the center of the ring

Thread color for the Bernese Mountain dog

☐ White
☐ Black

The rest of the parts are crocheted in a single color. For the Hokkaido and Japanese Shiba dogs, see their respective pages. For the Shih Tzu, wind the thread five times around a sheet of 0.38 in wide cardboard, then twist and attach it to the 2nd and 4th rows of the body with glue.

Magnets

See page 26.

Materials

[For all types of dogs]
Black or brown nose, 1 piece, 0.47 in
Round magnet, 1 piece, 1.57 in (diameter)
Synthetic cotton

[Pug]
Beige thread, 0.18 oz
Black thread, 0.14 oz
Clear plastic eyes, 2 pieces,
   0.35 in each each

[Beagle]
Brown thread, 0.25 oz
White thread, 0.11 oz
Black plastic sewing buttons, 2 pieces,
   0.24 in each

[Red Miniature Dachshund]
Brown thread, 0.28 oz
Dark brown thread, 0.07 oz
Black plastic sewing buttons, 2 pieces,
   0.24 in each

[Black and tan Miniature Dachshund]
Black thread, 0.25 oz
Brown thread, 0.07 oz
Brown plastic eyes, 2 pieces, 0.35 in each

[Welsh Corgi]
Beige mohair, 0.25 oz
White mohair, 0.11 oz
Black plastic sewing buttons, 2 pieces,
   0.24 in each

[Maltese]
White thread, 0.32 oz
Black plastic sewing buttons, 2 pieces,
   0.24 in each
Red felt, 2 sheets, 0.38 in x 0.58 in each

Tool

Crochet hook No. 4/0

Step-by-step method

1. Crochet each body part.
2. Cover the magnet with the face, and
pass the remaining thread through the
last row, tie and knot.
3. Attach the eyes to the face. Paint
the reverse side of the pug's eyes with
correction fluid.
4. Attach the nose to the mouth, and stuff
cotton in it.
5. Attach the mouth and the ears.

Face

Same for all types of dogs

Row	No. of stitches	
8	18	6 stitches
7	24	decrease per row
6	30	No increase or decrease
5	30	
4	24	6 stitches
3	18	increase per row
2	12	
1	6	Single crochet on the center of the ring

Pug's mouth

Row	No. of stitches	
4	19	2 stitches decrease
3	21	No increase or decrease
2	21	3 stitches increase
1	18	Single crochet around 7 chain stitches

Pug's ears

2 pieces

Row	No. of stitches	
4	12	2 stitches increase
3	10	3 stitches increase
2	7	2 stitches increase
1	5	Single crochet on the center of the ring

Welsh Corgi's ears

2 pieces

Row	No. of stitches	
6-5	12 each	No increase or decrease
4	12	2 stitches increase
3	10	3 stitches increase
2	7	2 stitches increase
1	5	Single crochet on the center of the ring

   Beige   White

c=center

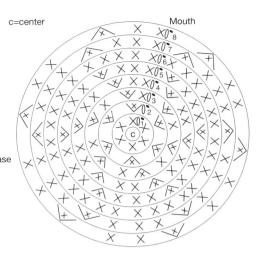

Mouth

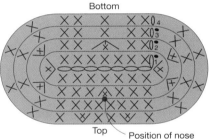

Bottom

Top — Position of nose

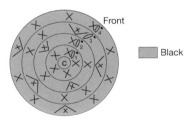

Front

   Black

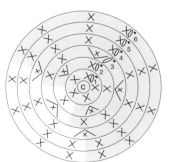

Ears of Miniature Dachshund and Beagle

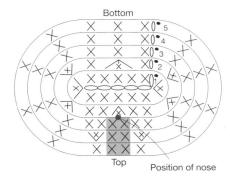

2 pieces

Row	No. of stitches	
6-5	6 each	No increase or decrease
4	6	3 stitches decrease
3	9	No increase or decrease
2	9	3 stitches increase
1	6	Single crochet on the center of the ring

Mouth for all dogs except the Pug

Bottom

Top

Position of nose

Row	No. of stitches	
5	15	No increase or decrease
4	15	2 stitches decrease
3	17	No increase or decrease
2	17	3 stitches increase
1	14	Single crochet around 5 chain stitches

Black for black and tan Miniature Dachshund

Brown for black and tan Miniature Dachshund

For all other dogs, use a single color.

Position of parts
Miniature Dachshund

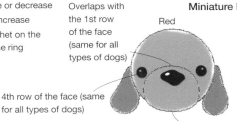

Red

Black and tan

Overlaps with the 1st row of the face (same for all types of dogs)

4th row of the face (same for all types of dogs)

5th row of the face (same for all types of dogs)

Embroider with brown thread after step 3 in the step-by-step method (for black and tan dog only).

5th and 6th row of the face (Attach it while pushing vertically.)

Pug

5 stitches

6th row of the face

Magnet

Do not hide the magnet when covering it with the face.

Beagle

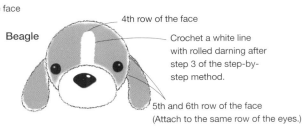

4th row of the face

Crochet a white line with rolled darning after step 3 of the step-by-step method.

5th and 6th row of the face (Attach to the same row of the eyes.)

Welsh Corgi

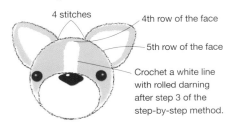

4 stitches

4th row of the face

5th row of the face

Crochet a white line with rolled darning after step 3 of the step-by-step method.

White line on the face
Beagle and Welsh Corgi

6 stitches with a single crochet around 5 chain stitches

Maltese

Attach the ears to the 6th row of the face slightly higher than the position of the eyes, then glue the ribbons to the ears.

The ears are crocheted in the same way as those of the Shih Tzu. Wind a piece of thread ten times around a sheet of 1.38 in wide cardboard.

Cellular Phone Accessories   See page 28.

Materials

[For all types of dogs]
Synthetic cotton
Double round ring, 1 piece, 0.2 in diameter
Strap with a lobster claw clasp

[Bernese Mountain Dog]
Black light thread, 0.21 oz
White thread, 0.11 oz
Brown thread, 0.07 oz
Red thread
Brown plastic eyes, 2 pieces, 0.24 in each
Black nose, 1 piece, 0.35 in

[Dalmatian]
White thread, 0.32 oz
Red thread
Black eyes, 2 pieces, 0.15 in each
Black nose, 1 piece, 0.35 in
Black wool felt

[Shih Tzu]
Gray thread, 0.21 oz
White thread, 0.11 oz
Red thread
Brown plastic eyes, 2 pieces, 0.24 in each
Black nose, 1 piece, 0.35 in
Red felt, 2 sheets, 0.38 in x 0.58 in.

[Jack Russell Terrier]
Brown light thread, 0.21 oz
White thread, 0.14 oz
Red thread
Black eyes, 2 pieces, 0.15 in each
Black nose, 1 piece, 0.35 in

[Chihuahua]
Beige thread, 0.07 oz
White thread, 0.07 oz
Red thread
Black plastic eyes, 2 pieces, 0.12 in each
Black nose, 1 piece, 0.18 in

[Japanese Shiba]
Black thread, 0.11 oz
White thread, 0.07 oz
Beige thread, 0.04 oz
Red thread
Brown plastic eyes, 2 pieces, 0.15 in each
Black nose, 1 piece, 0.18 in

[Hokkaido dog]
White thread, 0.18 oz
Red thread
Black eyes, 2 pieces, 0.12 in each
Black nose, 1 piece, 0.18 in

Tool

[Bernese Mountain dog, Dalmatian, Shih Tzu, Jack Russell Terrier]
Crochet hook No. 3/0
Crochet hook No. 2/0 (to crochet the legs, tails, and collars)

[Chihuahua, Japanese Shiba, Hokkaido dog]
Lacing needle No.2

Step-by-step method (for all types)

1. Crochet each body part. To make the head, see the corresponding diagrams for each dog. (The Shih Tzu's ears are made by winding thread 15 times around a sheet of 1.18 in wide cardboard.)
2. Stuff cotton inside the body (except for the legs).
3. Attach the body to the head.
4. Attach the legs and tail to the body.
5. Attach the ears to the head.
6. Make the collar by crocheting chain stitches in proportion to the neck circumference, then wind it around the neck, and stitch it up.
7. Crochet a double round ring on the head and attach a strap.

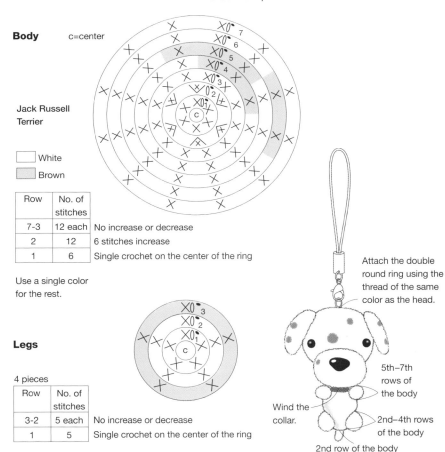

Body   c=center

Jack Russell Terrier

☐ White
▨ Brown

Row	No. of stitches	
7-3	12 each	No increase or decrease
2	12	6 stitches increase
1	6	Single crochet on the center of the ring

Use a single color for the rest.

Legs

4 pieces

Row	No. of stitches	
3-2	5 each	No increase or decrease
1	5	Single crochet on the center of the ring

▨ For the Chihuahua, Japanese Shiba, and Bernese Mountain dog, use the same color as the body. For the rest of the dogs, use only white.

Attach the double round ring using the thread of the same color as the head.

5th–7th rows of the body

Wind the collar.

2nd–4th rows of the body

2nd row of the body

See page 67 for the method of crocheting the tail.

Basic Crocheting

Slipknot

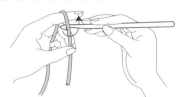 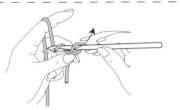

Chain stitch

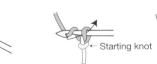

← Starting knot

← First stitch

3 stitches

The starting knot is not counted unless you are using a thick thread or crocheting for other special occasions.

Single crochet

1 stitch of starting chain

— Slipknot

Start to crochet from a starting chain. The starting chain is not included in the number of stitches.

The starting chain is not included in the number of stitches.

Single increase with a single crochet

  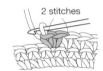

2 stitches

One stitch increase

Single decrease with a single crochet

One stitch decrease

Double decrease with a single crochet

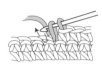

2 stitches decrease

Slip stitch

Mitsuki Hoshi

In 1999, Mitsuki, who likes Mickey Mouse very much, bought a Mickey Mouse crocheting kit, and that occasion became the start of her self-taught Amigurumi lessons. In the same year, her friend showed her a book written by an Amigurumi creator, which impressed her so much that she pursued the goal of becoming an Amigurumi creator herself, making everything from food to animals, and abiding by the motto "create everything with wool."

In 2002, she launched her website, which presents purely Amigurumi animals. Her works have frequently been presented in pet magazines. Currently, she also teaches a class on crocheting Amigurumi dogs.

http://hoshi-mitsuki.com/